Rhodes

Travel Guide 2024

The Ultimate Guide to Plan Your Perfect Trip with Accommodation, Things to Do, Insider Tips, and Dining Recommendations

Monica Friend

Content

Introduction

In the shimmering embrace of the Aegean Sea, where the sun caresses ancient stones and whispers secrets through olive groves, lies a timeless jewel: Rhodes. As I set foot on this enchanting island, a

wave of anticipation mingled with the salt-laden breeze, promising an odyssey of discovery.

Let me take you on a journey, a narrative woven with the threads of history, the warmth of the locals, and the tantalizing aromas of Mediterranean cuisine. Rhodes, an island steeped in myth and crowned with the remnants of knights and empires, unfolded before me like a treasure map waiting to be deciphered.

In the heart of Rhodes Town, where medieval walls echo tales of chivalry, I found myself lost in the labyrinth of cobblestone streets. Each step was a dance with the past, every turn revealing a new chapter in the island's storied history. As the grand Palace of the Grand Master loomed before me, its weathered stones whispered of conquests and triumphs, of knights who once walked these same paths.

Venturing beyond the walls, the landscape unfurled a vibrant tapestry of emerald hills and azure waters. The Valley of the Butterflies beckoned, a serene sanctuary where time slowed, and kaleidoscopic wings fluttered like confetti in a celebration of nature's beauty. The ancient city of Kamiros, with its hauntingly preserved ruins, spoke of a bygone era where whispers of daily life still lingered in the air.

Yet, Rhodes is not only a living museum but a haven for the senses. In the heart of the Old Town, the scent of souvlaki mingled with the sea breeze, drawing me to quaint tavernas where locals shared stories over glasses of robust red wine. Each bite was a communion with the island's flavors – olives plucked from age-old groves, feta that crumbled like history, and honey that tasted of sun-soaked blossoms.

As night fell, Rhodes transformed into a symphony of lights and laughter. The sound of bouzouki strings echoed through bustling alleys, inviting me to join the dance of life. From vibrant bars to seaside promenades, the island embraced me in its nocturnal embrace, promising memories that sparkled like constellations overhead.

This travel guide is not a mere compilation of facts; it is my attempt to share the heartbeat of Rhodes, to convey the emotions stirred by its beauty and the profound connection forged with its soul. Join me as we navigate the charming complexities of this island, unraveling its secrets and savoring every moment, for Rhodes is not just a destination – it is an immersive, transformative experience waiting to be embraced.

Fun facts About Rhodes

1. Rhodes was home to one of the Seven Wonders of the Ancient World: the Colossus of Rhodes.
2. Rhodes is the largest island in the Dodecanese archipelago.
3. The island is located in the southeastern Aegean Sea, just off the coast of Turkey.
4. Rhodes has a long and rich history, dating back to the Neolithic period.
5. The island was ruled by various empires over the centuries, including the Mycenaeans, the Persians, the Romans, and the Byzantines.
6. Rhodes is a popular tourist destination, known for its beautiful beaches, stunning scenery, and historical sites.
7. The capital of Rhodes is Rhodes City, a UNESCO World Heritage Site.

8. The city is surrounded by a medieval fortress, built by the Knights of St. John in the 14th century.

9. Rhodes is home to a number of interesting museums, including the Archaeological Museum, the Folklore Museum, and the Maritime Museum.

10. The island is also a popular spot for hiking, biking, and water sports.

11. Rhodes has a Mediterranean climate, with hot, dry summers and mild, wet winters.

12. The island is home to a number of unique plant and animal species, including the Rhodes butterfly.

13. Rhodes is a popular destination for weddings and honeymoons.

14. The island is also a popular filming location for movies and television shows.

15. Rhodes is a truly magical island that has something to offer everyone.

FAQs

1. What is the best time to visit Rhodes?

- The best time to visit Rhodes is during the shoulder seasons, from April to May or September to October. The weather is warm and sunny, but the crowds are smaller and the prices are lower.

2. How long should I stay in Rhodes?

- Most people spend 3-5 days on Rhodes. This is enough time to see the main sights and attractions and to relax on the beach.

3. What are the best things to do in Rhodes?

There are many things to do in Rhodes, including:

- Visiting the Acropolis of Lindos
- Exploring Rhodes Old Town
- Swimming in the crystal-clear waters of Anthony Quinn Bay
- Hiking in the Petaloudes Forest
- Taking a boat trip to the nearby islands of Symi and Chalki
- Going windsurfing or kitesurfing in Prasonisi

- Enjoying a traditional Greek meal in one of the many tavernas in Rhodes Town

4. Where should I stay in Rhodes?

- Rhodes has a wide variety of accommodation options to suit all budgets, from budget hostels to luxury resorts. The best place to stay depends on your personal preferences and budget.

5. What should I eat in Rhodes?

Rhodes has a delicious and varied cuisine. Some of the most popular dishes include:

- Moussaka
- Souvlaki
- Pastitsio
- Dolmadakia
- Spanakopita

6. How do I get around Rhodes?

- The best way to get around Rhodes is by renting a car or quad bike. There is also a public bus system, but it can be slow and unreliable.

7. What is the currency of Rhodes?

- The currency of Rhodes is the euro (€).

8. Do I need a visa to visit Rhodes?

- If you are a citizen of the European Union, you do not need a visa to visit Rhodes. However, if you are not a citizen of the European Union, you may need a visa.

9. What is the time zone in Rhodes?

- Rhodes is in Eastern European Time (EET), which is two hours ahead of Greenwich Mean Time (GMT).

10. What is the weather like in Rhodes?

- Rhodes has a Mediterranean climate, with hot, dry summers and mild, wet winters. The average temperature in July and August is 28 °C (82 °F), and the average temperature in January and February is 10 °C (50 °F).

11. Is Rhodes a safe place to visit?

- Yes, Rhodes is a safe place to visit. The crime rate is low, and the people are friendly and welcoming.

12. What should I pack for a trip to Rhodes?

Here are some packing tips for a trip to Rhodes:

- Clothes for hot weather, such as shorts, T-shirts, and sandals
- A swimsuit and cover-up
- A hat and sunglasses
- Sunscreen and insect repellent
- A camera
- A first-aid kit

13. What are some tips for traveling to Rhodes with children?

Here are some tips for traveling to Rhodes with children:

- Choose a family-friendly hotel or resort.
- Visit the Acropolis of Lindos with care, as there are many steep steps.
- Take plenty of breaks to avoid overexertion.
- Pack plenty of snacks and drinks.
- Be prepared for the sun, wind, and sand.

14. What are some sustainable travel tips for Rhodes?

Here are some sustainable travel tips for Rhodes:

- Rent a bike or car and explore the island on your own.
- Use public transportation whenever possible.
- Stay in an eco-friendly hotel or resort.
- Eat local, seasonal food.

15. What is the nightlife like in Rhodes?

- Rhodes has a lively nightlife scene, especially in Rhodes Town. There are bars and clubs to suit all tastes, from traditional Greek tavernas to trendy cocktail bars.

16. What are some of the best souvenirs to bring back from Rhodes?

Some of the best souvenirs to bring back from Rhodes include:

- Olive oil and other local produce
- Jewelry made from local materials, such as silver and gold
- Traditional Greek clothing and accessories

- Souvenirs from the Acropolis of Lindos and other historical sites

17. What are some of the best places to shop in Rhodes?

There are many great places to shop in Rhodes, including:

- The Old Town of Rhodes is home to a variety of shops selling souvenirs, handicrafts, and jewelry.
- The New Town of Rhodes has a wider selection of shops, including international brands and department stores.
- The villages of Rhodes have a more traditional shopping experience.

18. Are there any festivals or events that take place in Rhodes?

Yes, there are many festivals and events that take place in Rhodes throughout the year. Some of the most popular include:

- The Rhodes Festival takes place in July and August and features a variety of music, dance, and theater performances.

- The Feast of the Assumption of the Virgin Mary, which takes place on August 15th and is celebrated with religious processions and festivities.
- The Rhodes Wine Festival, which takes place in September and showcases the island's best wines.

19. What are some of the best beaches in Rhodes?

Rhodes has many beautiful beaches to choose from, including:

- Agia Marina Beach is a long sandy beach with crystal-clear waters.
- Anthony Quinn Bay is a secluded cove with stunning cliffs.
- Faliraki Beach is a lively beach with bars, restaurants, and water sports.
- Tsambika Beach is a popular beach with soft sand and shallow waters.
- Lindos Beach is a picturesque beach with a backdrop of ancient ruins.

20. What are some tips for saving money on a trip to Rhodes?

Here are some tips for saving money on a trip to Rhodes:

- Travel during the shoulder seasons, when prices are lower.
- Stay in a budget-friendly hotel or apartment.
- Eat at local tavernas and cafes, which offer good value for money.
- Take advantage of free activities, such as hiking and swimming.
- Use public transportation whenever possible.
- Rent a car or bike to explore the island on your own.
- Pack light to avoid baggage fees.

Destination Overview

A Glimpse of Rhodes

Nestled in the embrace of the southeastern Aegean Sea, Rhodes emerges as a captivating mosaic of history, natural beauty, and vibrant culture. This sun-kissed island, the largest of the Dodecanese archipelago, invites travelers into a world where antiquity and modernity harmonize seamlessly. As you step onto its shores, prepare to be enraptured by a destination that transcends time.

Geography:

Rhodes, with an area of approximately 1,400 square kilometers, boasts a diverse topography that effortlessly blends the coastal allure of pristine beaches with the rugged charm of rolling hills. The island's centerpiece is the imposing Mount Attavyros, standing at 1,215 meters, offering panoramic vistas that stretch across the turquoise expanse of the Aegean.

Stretching out from the mountainous spine, fertile valleys carpeted with vineyards and olive groves paint a picturesque scene. The island's coastline, adorned with golden sands and crystalline waters, beckons beach enthusiasts and water lovers alike. Rhodes' geographical diversity ensures that every traveler finds their niche, whether amid the tranquility of the countryside or the bustling energy of coastal towns.

Climate:

Blessed by the Mediterranean climate, Rhodes unveils a symphony of sunshine and warmth throughout the year. Summers, extending from June to September, deliver an average of 12 hours of daily sunlight, transforming the island into a haven for sun-seekers. Winters, mild and short-lived, maintain a comfortable temperature, making Rhodes a year-round destination.

The gentle sea breezes mitigate the summer heat, creating an ideal atmosphere for exploration. Evenings become a celebration of al fresco dining under starlit skies, a quintessential Rhodes experience. Whether you choose to bask in the summer glow or embrace the island's serene winter charm, Rhodes promises a climate that complements every traveler's desire.

Historical Significance

Rhodes, a living testament to the epochs that have shaped the Mediterranean world, stands as a witness to the passage of civilizations. The island's narrative dates back to ancient times when the Colossus of Rhodes, one of the Seven Wonders of the Ancient World, presided over its harbor. Traces of Greek, Roman, Byzantine, and Ottoman influences weave through the cobblestone streets, archaeological sites, and medieval fortifications.

The medieval city of Rhodes, a UNESCO World Heritage Site, encapsulates the island's historical grandeur. Encircled by towering medieval walls, this labyrinthine enclave showcases Gothic architecture, Byzantine churches, and palaces that echo with tales of knights and crusaders. The Street of the Knights, lined with imposing inns, transports visitors to an era when chivalry reigned supreme.

From the ancient acropolis of Kamiros to the archaeological wonders of Lindos, Rhodes stands as an open-air museum where each stone whispers tales of conquests, trade, and cultural exchanges. This historical richness, layered like the strata of its ancient soil, transforms every corner of Rhodes into a portal to the past.

In this destination overview, we have barely scratched the surface of Rhodes' allure. As you embark on your journey through this multifaceted island, be prepared to uncover the layers of history, soak in the natural splendors, and embrace the cultural tapestry that defines Rhodes.

Visa and Entry Requirements

International Visitors

Before packing your bags, it's crucial to check the visa and entry requirements for your nationality. Most visitors from EU countries, the United States, Canada, Australia, and many other nations enjoy visa-free entry for stays of up to 90 days. However, it's wise to confirm this information with the Greek embassy or consulate in your home country.

Passport Validity:

Ensure your passport is valid for at least six months beyond your planned departure date. It's a small detail that can save you from unnecessary hassles upon arrival.

Extended Stays:

If you're considering a stay longer than 90 days or for specific purposes such as work or study, it's advisable to contact the Greek embassy in advance to determine the necessary steps and requirements.

Best Time to Visit

Peak Season (June to September)

The summer months, from June to September, constitute the peak tourist season. During this period, Rhodes basks in abundant sunshine, and the island's vibrant energy comes to life. Beach enthusiasts, water sports enthusiasts, and sunseekers will find this time ideal for enjoying the crystal-clear waters and warm Mediterranean climate.

Shoulder Seasons (April to May, October)

For those seeking a balance between pleasant weather and fewer crowds, the shoulder seasons of April to May and October are optimal. Temperatures are mild, and the island exudes a tranquil charm. This is an ideal time for cultural exploration, outdoor activities, and unhurried sightseeing.

Winter (November to March)

While winter in Rhodes is mild compared to many other European destinations, it is the quietest season. Travelers looking for solitude, unique local experiences, and a more intimate connection with the island's culture may find winter appealing. It's essential to note that some tourist facilities may operate on reduced schedules during this time.

Travel Essentials Checklist

Embarking on your Rhodes adventure requires thoughtful preparation to ensure a smooth and enjoyable journey. Here's a comprehensive travel essentials checklist to guide you through the preparations:

Before You Go:

1. Passport and Visa: Ensure your passport is valid for at least six months beyond your planned departure date. Check the visa requirements for your nationality and obtain any necessary visas.

2. Travel Insurance: Invest in comprehensive travel insurance that covers medical emergencies, trip cancellations, and lost or stolen belongings.

3. Health Precautions: Consult your healthcare provider for any necessary vaccinations or health precautions. Bring a small first aid kit for minor ailments.

4. Currency: Familiarize yourself with the local currency (Euro) and inform your bank of your travel dates to avoid any issues with card transactions.

5. Electrical Adapters: Check the electrical outlets in Rhodes and bring the appropriate adapters for your devices.

Packing Essentials:

1. Light Clothing: Rhodes enjoys a Mediterranean climate, so pack lightweight and breathable clothing suitable for warm weather.

2. Comfortable Footwear: Comfortable walking shoes are essential, especially if you plan to explore historical sites or embark on nature trails.

3. Sun Protection: Pack sunscreen, sunglasses, and a hat to shield yourself from the Mediterranean sun.

4. Swimwear: Don't forget your swimsuit for enjoying the beautiful beaches and crystal-clear waters.

5. Reusable Water Bottle: Stay hydrated during your explorations by carrying a reusable water bottle.

On-the-Go Essentials:

1. Daypack: A small daypack is handy for carrying essentials during day trips and explorations.

2. Travel Guidebook: Bring a travel guidebook for insights into local culture, history, and recommended attractions.

3. Language Translator: Consider a language translation app or a basic phrasebook to facilitate communication.
4. Portable Charger: Keep your devices charged with a portable charger, especially during long days of exploration.
5. Travel Documents: Organize your travel documents, including flight tickets, accommodation reservations, and any required permits.

What to Avoid:
1. Overpacking: Rhodes has a relaxed atmosphere, and casual attire is generally suitable. Avoid overpacking by focusing on versatile clothing.
2. Excessive Valuables: Leave unnecessary valuables at home to reduce the risk of loss or theft. Use a money belt or hidden pouch for essential documents.
3. Disregarding Local Customs: Respect local customs and traditions. Dress modestly

when visiting religious sites and be mindful of cultural sensitivities.

4. Neglecting Sun Safety: The Mediterranean sun can be intense. Avoid sunburn by applying sunscreen regularly and seeking shade during peak hours.

5. Unofficial Guides: When exploring historical sites, rely on official guides to ensure accurate information and a deeper understanding of the site's significance.

By adhering to this checklist and being mindful of what to avoid, you're poised to make the most of your Rhodes adventure. Prepare to immerse yourself in the island's beauty, culture, and history, all while navigating with confidence and ease.

Getting Around

Navigating the captivating landscapes of Rhodes is an integral part of your adventure, and the island offers a myriad of efficient transportation options for stress-free travel.

Getting to Rhodes:

Embarking on your Rhodes adventure is an exhilarating journey, and the island's accessibility ensures a smooth transition from anticipation to exploration. The primary gateway to Rhodes is the Diagoras International Airport (RHO), located just 14 kilometers southwest of Rhodes Town. Serving as a hub for both domestic and international flights, this modern airport welcomes travelers with open arms.

International Flights:
Rhodes enjoys direct connections with major European cities, including London, Berlin, Rome, and Moscow. Airlines such as Aegean Airlines,

British Airways, and Ryanair operate regular flights during the peak travel seasons, facilitating convenient access for global visitors.

Domestic Flights:
For those exploring Greece beyond Rhodes, domestic flights connect the island to Athens and Thessaloniki. These short flights provide a seamless link between Rhodes and the cultural and historical treasures of the mainland.

Navigating the Airport:
Upon landing at Diagoras International Airport, the efficiency of the airport's design ensures a swift transition from the runway to your Rhodes experience.

Immigration and Customs:
Navigating immigration and customs is a streamlined process. Ensure you have your passport, visa (if required), and any necessary

documents readily accessible. Greek hospitality awaits just beyond the customs gates.

Transportation from the Airport:
Various transportation options await to whisk you away to your destination. Taxis, readily available at designated taxi ranks, offer a hassle-free way to reach your accommodation. Alternatively, car rental services provide the freedom to explore the island at your own pace.

Airport Facilities:
Diagoras International Airport boasts modern facilities, including duty-free shops, cafes, and currency exchange services. Whether you need to grab a quick bite or indulge in some pre-flight shopping, the airport caters to your needs.

Efficient Modes of Transportation:

1. Car Rentals:
- Freedom of Exploration: Renting a car provides the ultimate freedom to explore

Rhodes at your own pace. The island boasts well-maintained roads, and the scenic drives are a delight.

- Rental Tips: Choose a reliable rental agency, book in advance during peak seasons, and familiarize yourself with local traffic rules.

2. Public Buses:

- Cost-Effective Travel: Rhodes has an extensive bus network connecting major towns and tourist destinations. It's a budget-friendly option for those who prefer public transportation.
- Central Bus Station: The central bus station in Rhodes Town is the hub for island-wide routes, making it convenient for planning day trips or venturing to various attractions.

3. Taxis:

- Convenient and Accessible: Taxis are readily available in urban centers and tourist hubs, offering a convenient mode of transportation for specific destinations or areas with limited public transit.

- Fare Information: Confirm the fare before starting your journey, and it's customary to tip drivers.

4. Scooter and Bike Rentals:

- Eco-Friendly Exploration: Renting a scooter or bike provides a fun and eco-friendly way to navigate Rhodes' narrow streets, discover hidden gems, and enjoy the island's breeze.

5. Boats and Ferries:

- Island Hopping: If you're keen on exploring nearby islands or taking day trips, boats and ferries offer a scenic and enjoyable means of transportation.

Exploring Rhodes by Car, Bus, and More:

1. Exploring by Car:

- Scenic Drives: With a car, venture off the beaten path to discover secluded beaches, charming villages, and panoramic viewpoints.

- Parking Tips: Be mindful of parking regulations, especially in Rhodes Town, and utilize designated parking areas.

2. Bus Adventures:

- Comfortable Journeys: Buses are air-conditioned and offer a comfortable means of travel. Plan your day trips by checking the bus schedules in advance.
- Scenic Routes: Some bus routes traverse scenic routes, providing passengers with picturesque views of the island's landscapes.

3. Tips for Stress-Free Travel:

- Plan Ahead:

- Itinerary Preparation: Plan your daily itinerary, considering the mode of transportation that best suits each destination.
- Timetables: Familiarize yourself with bus schedules, especially if relying on public transportation.

- Stay Informed:
  - Local Updates: Stay informed about any transportation updates, especially if you plan to use buses, which may be subject to schedule changes.
- Respect Local Customs:
  - Taxis: If using taxis, be aware that there may be shared rides, and it's customary to share a taxi with other passengers going in the same direction.
- Be Flexible:
  - Embrace the Adventure: Unexpected detours or changes in plans are part of the adventure. Embrace the flexibility of your journey and enjoy the discoveries along the way.

Rhodes, with its diverse transportation options, invites you to embark on a seamless exploration of its wonders. Whether you choose the flexibility of a rental car, the convenience of buses, or the charm of scooters, each mode of transportation adds a unique layer to your Rhodes adventure. So, buckle up, relax, and get ready to traverse this enchanting island with ease.

Accommodation

Finding the perfect accommodation is a pivotal part of crafting an unforgettable Rhodes experience. From luxurious resorts to cozy guesthouses, the island caters to every taste and budget, ensuring

your stay feels like a true home away from home.

Finding Your Home Away from Home:

1. Rhodes Town:

- Historical Charms: Stay within the medieval walls of Rhodes Town for a unique blend of history and modern conveniences. Charming boutique hotels and guesthouses dot the narrow cobblestone streets.

2. Ixia and Ialyssos:

- Beachfront Bliss: If you crave the calming whispers of the Aegean, consider accommodations in Ixia or Ialyssos. These coastal areas offer a range of hotels with breathtaking sea views.

3. Faliraki:

- Vibrant Vibes: For those seeking lively nightlife and a vibrant atmosphere, Faliraki is a bustling resort town with a variety of accommodations, from budget-friendly to more upscale options.

4. Lindos:

- Picturesque Retreat: Nestled between rocky cliffs and the sea, Lindos offers a postcard-perfect setting. Boutique hotels and traditional villas enhance the picturesque allure of this charming village.

Accommodation Options for Every Budget:

1. Luxury Resorts:

- Elegance and Opulence: Indulge in the lavish offerings of luxury resorts, where five-star amenities, spa services, and panoramic views of the Aegean create a cocoon of opulence.

2. Boutique Hotels:

- Charm and Character: Boutique hotels in Rhodes Town and beyond are known for their unique character, personalized service, and often, a fusion of modern comforts with historical elements.

3. Budget-Friendly Choices:

- Affordable Comfort: Budget-conscious travelers can find a range of comfortable accommodations, including guesthouses, hostels, and family-run hotels that provide a warm and welcoming atmosphere.

4. Apartments and Villas:

- Home-like Independence: Apartments and villas offer the freedom of self-catering and are ideal for those seeking a more private and independent stay. They are scattered across the island, providing a home-like experience.

Noteworthy Hotels and Resorts:

1. Atrium Platinum Luxury Resort Hotel & Spa:
   - Contemporary Elegance: Situated in Ixia, this modern resort offers spacious rooms, a state-of-the-art spa, and multiple dining options. The architecture seamlessly blends with the natural surroundings.

2.. Amathus Beach Hotel Rhodes:

- Luxury by the Sea: This five-star resort in Ixia boasts lavish rooms, multiple pools, and direct access to a private beach. Fine dining and spa facilities elevate the guest experience.

3. Melenos Lindos Hotel:

- Timeless Elegance: In the heart of Lindos, Melenos Lindos Hotel exudes timeless elegance with its meticulous design and breathtaking views. Each room is a sanctuary of comfort and style.

4. Elakati Luxury Boutique Hotel:

- Urban Chic in Rhodes Town: This boutique hotel in Rhodes Town combines urban chic with historic charm. Rooftop terraces provide panoramic views, and the stylish interiors showcase modern Greek design.

As you embark on your journey to Rhodes, let your choice of accommodation enhance the magic of your stay. Whether you prefer the opulence of a luxury resort, the charm of a boutique hotel, or the coziness of a budget-friendly option, Rhodes opens its doors to ensure your accommodation feels like a sanctuary amid the Aegean wonders. Your home away from home awaits, promising not just a place to rest but a vital part of your Rhodes adventure.

Food And Dining

Embark on a culinary journey that tantalizes your taste buds and immerses you in the rich flavors of Rhodes. From traditional delicacies to contemporary gastronomy, the island's cuisine is a celebration of local ingredients and culinary craftsmanship.

Savoring Rhodes Cuisine:

1. Influences and Traditions:

- Mediterranean Melting Pot: Rhodes' cuisine reflects a delightful fusion of Mediterranean influences, with nods to Greek, Turkish, and

Italian flavors. Expect an array of dishes showcasing fresh produce, olive oil, and aromatic herbs.

2. Local Ingredients:
   - Bounty of the Land and Sea: Rhodes' fertile soil and the surrounding azure waters contribute to a diverse array of ingredients. Fresh seafood, locally sourced vegetables, and aromatic herbs are staples in the island's kitchens.

3. Hospitality Culture:
   - Warmth on a Plate: Beyond the ingredients, Rhodes' culinary experience is characterized by warm hospitality. Local tavernas and family-run restaurants welcome guests with open arms, ensuring that each meal feels like a shared celebration.

A Culinary Journey Through Local Flavors:

1. Mezedes (Appetizers):
   - Small Bites, Big Flavor: Start your culinary journey with mezedes – an array of

appetizers that include dolmades (grape leaves stuffed with rice), tzatziki, and melitzanosalata (eggplant dip).

2. Souvlaki and Gyro:
   - Grilled Perfection: Indulge in the quintessential Greek street food – souvlaki. Skewers of grilled meat, often served in pita bread with tomatoes, onions, and tzatziki, offer a burst of smoky goodness.
3. Fresh Seafood:
   - From Sea to Plate: Enjoy the bounty of the Aegean with fresh seafood dishes. Try grilled octopus, marinated anchovies, or a classic seafood risotto for an authentic taste of Rhodes.
4. Kleftiko:
   - Slow-Cooked Delight: This traditional dish involves slow-cooking lamb with garlic, lemon, and local herbs until it becomes melt-in-your-mouth tender. A culinary journey back in time.

5. Baklava and Loukoumades:

- Sweet Endings: Conclude your meal with a touch of sweetness. Baklava, layers of filo pastry with nuts and honey, and loukoumades, Greek doughnuts drizzled with honey, are irresistible treats.

Must-Try Dishes and Beverages:

1. Pitaroudia:

- Chickpea Fritters: A local specialty, pitaroudia are chickpea fritters infused with local herbs, a delicious vegetarian option bursting with flavor.

2. Pastitsio:

- Greek Lasagna: This baked pasta dish with layers of minced meat and béchamel sauce is a comforting and hearty choice for those seeking a taste of traditional Greek cuisine.

3. Rhodian Wine:

- Vineyard Elegance: Rhodes boasts a burgeoning wine scene. Sample local varieties like Athiri and Mandilaria, or explore the island's wineries for a vineyard tour and tasting.

4. Souma:

- Spirit of the Island: Souma, a traditional Rhodian spirit, is distilled from grapes and flavored with anise. Sip it slowly to savor the essence of the island.

Rhodes' culinary landscape is a symphony of flavors, a journey that transcends the mere act of eating. Each dish tells a story, a narrative woven from centuries of tradition and a passion for exquisite ingredients. As you embark on your gastronomic odyssey in Rhodes, prepare to be enchanted by the tastes and aromas that linger, creating memories as enduring as the island itself.

Activities and Attractions

Prepare to embark on a journey of discovery as Rhodes unfolds its myriad activities and attractions. From ancient wonders to hidden gems, the island

beckons with unforgettable experiences that promise to etch lasting memories.

Unforgettable Experiences Await:

1. Explore the Medieval City:

- Time-Travel in Rhodes Town: Wander through the medieval streets of Rhodes Town, a UNESCO World Heritage Site. The

Palace of the Grand Master, Street of the Knights, and the Archaeological Museum invite you to step back in time.

2. Discover Lindos:

- Iconic Acropolis Views: Climb the donkey-laden paths or opt for a more modern approach by foot to reach the Acropolis of Lindos. The panoramic views of the azure sea and the white-washed village below are breathtaking.

3. Valley of the Butterflies:

- Nature's Spectacle: Visit the Valley of the Butterflies in Petaloudes during the summer months when thousands of butterflies gather. The lush valley and cascading waterfalls create a serene setting for a tranquil escape.

Must-Visit Landmarks:

1. Ancient Kamiros:

- Ruins by the Sea: Explore the well-preserved ruins of Ancient Kamiros, an ancient city frozen in time. The agora, temples, and houses offer a glimpse into daily life in antiquity.

2. Monolithos Castle:

- A Castle in the Sky: Perched atop a rocky hill, Monolithos Castle provides not only historical intrigue but also stunning panoramic views of the island and the Aegean Sea.

-

3. Seven Springs:

- Nature's Oasis: Find shade in the verdant surroundings of Seven Springs, a natural oasis dotted with crystal-clear springs. Take a refreshing walk through the lush forest and cross the wooden bridge for a serene escape.

Hidden Gems Off the Beaten Path:

1. Kritinia Castle:

- **Castle with a View:** Venture to Kritinia Castle for a quieter alternative to the more famous landmarks. The medieval ruins offer a peaceful atmosphere and stunning vistas of the coastline.

2. Filerimos Hill:

- **Spiritual Retreat:** Ascend Filerimos Hill to explore the Monastery of Filerimos and the iconic Golgotha path. The sweeping views and serene atmosphere make it a hidden gem for those seeking a spiritual retreat.

3. Tsambika Monastery:

- Clifftop Sanctuary: Visit Tsambika Monastery perched on a hilltop. Legend has it that the barren are blessed with fertility after climbing the 300 steps leading to the monastery. The panoramic views are a bonus.

Rhodes, a treasure trove of history and natural wonders, invites you to uncover its hidden gems and iconic landmarks. Whether you're wandering the medieval streets of Rhodes Town, climbing ancient acropolises, or discovering tranquil oases, each step is a revelation. The island's rich tapestry of activities and attractions ensures that every traveler finds their path to awe and wonder on this enchanting journey. Let Rhodes captivate your senses and ignite your spirit with experiences that linger long after the journey is complete.

Things to Do

Welcome to Rhodes, a haven of history, sun-soaked beaches, and endless exploration. Brace yourself for a whirlwind of activities that will make your journey through this Aegean jewel an unforgettable odyssey.

Explore the Enchanting Old Town:

Palace of the Grand Master:

- Step into History: Wander through the medieval marvel that is the Palace of the Grand Master. Marvel at the intricate mosaic floors and imagine the echoes of knights from centuries past.

Street of the Knights (Ippoton):

- Time-Travel Stroll: Take a stroll along the cobbled Street of the Knights. Each step is a journey through time, surrounded by well-preserved medieval architecture and hidden courtyards.

Archaeological Museum of Rhodes:

- Ancient Wonders: Dive into Rhodes' rich history at the Archaeological Museum. From classical sculptures to artifacts dating back to antiquity, this museum is a treasure trove for history enthusiasts.

Bask in the Sun at Idyllic Beaches:

Tsambika Beach:

- Golden Sands: Sink your toes into the golden sands of Tsambika Beach. With crystal-clear waters and a backdrop of hills, it's a serene escape for sunbathing and water activities.

Lindos Beach:

- Classic Elegance: Lindos Beach, with its turquoise waters and views of the Acropolis, is a postcard-perfect spot. Enjoy the sun, swim, and indulge in seaside delights at local tavernas.

Uncover Nature's Beauty:

Valley of the Butterflies (Petaloudes):

- Nature's Spectacle: Witness a breathtaking display at the Valley of the Butterflies. In the summer, thousands of butterflies create a mesmerizing dance among the lush greenery.

Seven Springs (Epta Piges):

- Refreshing Oasis: Escape to the Seven Springs, a natural oasis shaded by plane trees. Wander through the tunnels, feel the cool mist, and enjoy a picnic in this tranquil haven.

Adventure and Activities:

Water Sports in Faliraki:

- Adrenaline Rush: For thrill-seekers, Faliraki is a paradise. Try your hand at water sports like jet-skiing or parasailing, and let the turquoise waves become your playground.

Hiking in Profitis Ilias:

- Panoramic Views: Lace up your hiking boots for an ascent to Profitis Ilias. The panoramic views from the island's highest point are a rewarding spectacle for nature enthusiasts.

Immerse Yourself in Local Culture:

Rhodes Summer Festival:

- Cultural Extravaganza: If your visit aligns with summer, don't miss the Rhodes Summer Festival. From concerts to theatrical performances, it's a celebration of arts against the backdrop of historical venues.

Local Markets - Agora:

- Shop Like a Local: Dive into the bustling Agora markets. Sample local produce, snag handmade souvenirs, and let the vibrant atmosphere immerse you in Rhodesian daily life.

Rhodes beckons with a myriad of activities that cater to every taste. Whether you're a history buff, a sun seeker, or an adventurer, the island unfolds a kaleidoscope of experiences. Let each day be a new chapter, and as you navigate this Aegean paradise, may your Rhodesian adventure be as diverse and vibrant as the island itself. Enjoy every moment!

Entertainment and Nightlife

As the sun dips below the horizon, Rhodes transforms into a realm of evening enchantment, offering a vibrant tapestry of entertainment and nightlife. From lively bars to cultural shows, the island pulsates with nocturnal delights that promise to extend your adventure well into the night.

Evening Delights on Rhodes

1. Rhodes Town by Night:

- Illuminated Majesty: Take a leisurely stroll through Rhodes Town as the medieval architecture comes alive with enchanting illumination. The Grand Master's Palace and the Street of the Knights exude a timeless charm under the night sky.

2. Mandraki Harbor:

- Seaside Serenity: Visit Mandraki Harbor and enjoy a peaceful evening by the sea. The illuminated deer and doe sculptures at the entrance create a magical atmosphere as you explore the waterfront.

3. Sunset Views:

- Dine with a View: Experience the breathtaking sunset views from one of the seaside restaurants in Rhodes Town or Lindos. The warm hues of the setting sun create a picturesque backdrop for a delightful evening.

Bars, Clubs, and Cultural Shows

1. Bar-Hopping in Rhodes Town:

- Cocktails and Conversations: Dive into the lively bar scene in Rhodes Town. From chic cocktail lounges to traditional Greek tavernas, the Old Town offers a diverse range of options for every taste.

2. Lindos Nightlife:

- Under the Stars: Lindos, with its rooftop bars and seaside venues, provides a more intimate setting for a night out. Enjoy a cocktail with the Acropolis as your backdrop or dance under the stars.

3. Cultural Shows:

- Theatrical Extravaganza: Immerse yourself in the island's cultural heritage with traditional Greek dance and music performances. Various venues host cultural shows, providing insight into Rhodes' rich history and traditions.

4. Nightclubs in Faliraki:

- Electric Energy: For those seeking a more energetic atmosphere, Faliraki boasts a vibrant nightlife scene with nightclubs playing a mix of international and Greek music, ensuring an unforgettable night of dancing and celebration.

Nighttime Attractions

1. Kallithea Springs:

- Moonlit Springs: Experience the romantic allure of Kallithea Springs after dark. The beautifully illuminated rotunda and the therapeutic springs create a serene and magical ambiance.

2. Nighttime Boat Tours:

- Aegean Nightscape: Join a nighttime boat tour to witness the island from a different perspective. The twinkling lights along the coastline and the moonlit sea create a mesmerizing tableau.

3. Rhodes Casino:

- Gaming and Entertainment: For those feeling lucky, the Casino of Rhodes offers an elegant venue for an evening of gaming and entertainment. Test your luck at the tables or enjoy a sophisticated drink at the bar.

Rhodes' nightlife is a symphony of experiences, each note contributing to an unforgettable nocturnal melody. Whether you prefer the intimate charm of seaside bars, the vibrant energy of nightclubs, or the cultural richness of traditional shows, the island caters to every whim. As the stars emerge overhead, let Rhodes be your stage for a night of entertainment and revelry, ensuring that your adventure extends far beyond the daylight hours.

Shopping

Indulge in the art of retail therapy as Rhodes unveils a world of shopping delights. From quaint boutiques to bustling markets, the island invites you to discover unique treasures and bring home a piece of its vibrant culture.

Retail Therapy on the Island

1. Rhodes Old Town Bazaars:
   - Historical Treasures: Navigate the cobblestone streets of Rhodes Old Town, where a myriad of bazaars beckon. Find handmade jewelry, leather goods, and traditional ceramics in the shadow of medieval architecture.
2. New Town Shopping Streets:
   - Modern Elegance: Explore the modern side of Rhodes in the New Town, where chic boutiques and contemporary stores line bustling streets. Fashion, accessories, and

local designer items await discerning shoppers.

3. Lindos Boutique Shops:

- Coastal Elegance: Lindos, with its charming white-washed buildings, offers an array of boutique shops with a coastal flair. Discover stylish resort wear, handmade crafts, and unique souvenirs.

Unique Souvenirs to Bring Home

1. Rhodian Ceramics:

- Artistry in Clay: Immerse yourself in the island's rich pottery tradition with Rhodian ceramics. Bring home hand-painted plates, bowls, and decorative items that showcase the craftsmanship of local artisans.

2. Olive Wood Products:

- Nature's Elegance: Explore the rustic beauty of olive wood products, from intricately carved utensils to elegant serving platters. These timeless pieces embody the essence of Rhodes.

3. Local Wines and Spirits:

- A Toast to Rhodes: Visit local wineries or specialty shops to procure bottles of Rhodian wines or the island's traditional spirits, such as souma or mastiha liqueur, offering a taste of the Aegean.

4. Lace and Embroidery:

- Timeless Craftsmanship: Delight in the delicate artistry of Rhodes' lace and embroidery. Handcrafted linens, tablecloths, and clothing items showcase the island's timeless craftsmanship.

Popular Shopping Districts

1. Sokratous Street, Rhodes Town:

- Historic Stroll: Sokratous Street, in the heart of Rhodes Old Town, is a shopper's paradise. From antique stores to contemporary boutiques, it offers a blend of history and modernity.

2. Ermou Street, Rhodes Town:

- Modern Elegance: Ermou Street, in the New Town, is a hub of modern shopping. Explore international brands, local designers, and charming cafes for a leisurely shopping experience.

3. Panetiou Street, Lindos:

- Seaside Charm: Panetiou Street in Lindos offers a mix of souvenir shops, boutiques, and art galleries against the backdrop of the Acropolis. Stroll through this picturesque street for a leisurely shopping spree.

Rhodes' shopping scene is a delightful mosaic of tradition and contemporary flair. Whether you're weaving through the labyrinthine streets of the Old Town, exploring modern avenues in the New Town, or indulging in coastal elegance in Lindos, each corner of the island offers a unique shopping experience. As you peruse the treasures of Rhodes, let each find tell a story, creating a tapestry of memories that will forever connect you to the allure of this Aegean gem.

Itinerary

DAY 1

Discover the Medieval City

Morning: Begin your day at the awe-inspiring Palace of the Grand Master of the Knights of Rhodes. Dive into medieval history as you explore the Knights' legacy. Follow it up with a leisurely stroll along the charming Street of the Knights, surrounded by medieval wonders.

Afternoon: Savor authentic Greek flavors at Tamam, a traditional eatery. Continue your historical journey at the Archaeological Museum of Rhodes, which houses a captivating collection of ancient artifacts.

Evening: Head to Bardakos for a cozy dinner, then take a sunset walk around Mandraki Harbour. Conclude the night with a drink at Mavrikos, a lively bar known for its delightful cocktails.
Bedtime: Find your perfect stay in Rhodes, Greece.

DAY 2
Natural Wonders and Beach Bliss

Morning: Venture on a day trip to Seven Springs, a serene oasis embraced by nature. Wander through shaded paths, discovering hidden springs. Later, bask in the sun at Tsambika Beach.

Afternoon: Enjoy a beachside lunch at Mavrias Village, relishing traditional Greek cuisine with

Aegean Sea views. Visit the Valley of the Butterflies, a unique reserve where butterflies are enchanted among the trees.

Evening: Dive into seafood delights at Artemis. Follow it with a leisurely stroll along the illuminated Medieval City of Rhodes.

Bedtime: Find your perfect stay in Rhodes, Greece.

DAY 3
Island Escape to Symi

Morning: Hop on a high-speed boat to Symi Island. Explore the vibrant town, uncovering its history at Kahal Shalom Synagogue and Rhodes Jewish Museum.

Afternoon: Delight in lunch at Taste of India, offering Indian cuisine with a harbor view. Take a boat trip to St. Paul's Bay, surrounded by awe-inspiring cliffs.

Evening: Experience a sunset cruise with Rhodes Sunset Cruise, enjoying unlimited drinks and a Greek barbecue dinner.

Bedtime: Find your perfect stay in Symi Island, Greece.

DAY 4
Ancient Ruins and Sandy Shores

Morning: Take a bus to the Acropolis of Lindos. Marvel at ancient ruins perched on a hilltop.

Afternoon: Relish lunch at To Marouli, a restaurant blending tradition with modern twists. Relax at Afandou Beach, a sandy haven.

Evening: Explore Monolithos Castle with panoramic views. Cap off the day with a seafood feast at Mavrikos.

Bedtime: Find your perfect stay in Lindos, Greece.

DAY 5
Rhodes' Highlights

Morning: Begin at the Acropolis of Rhodes, soaking in panoramic views. Explore the Medieval City's charming streets.

Afternoon: Enjoy lunch at Tamam. Visit Ancient Kamiros, revealing the city's ancient remnants.

Evening: Delight in dinner at Bardakos, stroll around Mandraki Harbour, and end the trip with a drink at Tamam.

Bedtime: Find your perfect stay in Rhodes, Greece.

Day Trip from Rhodes

Rhodes, an island of enchantment, also serves as a gateway to neighboring wonders. Embark on day trips that transport you to nearby islands and the mainland, adding layers of discovery to your Aegean adventure.

Exploring Nearby Islands and Mainland

1. Symi - A Colorful Escape:

- Vibrant Harbor Town: Set sail to Symi, a picturesque island known for its vibrant harbor lined with neoclassical buildings. Explore the Monastery of the Archangel Michael and indulge in fresh seafood at a waterfront taverna.

2. Lindos - Acropolis and Azure Waters:

- Historic Beauty: Venture to Lindos, where the ancient Acropolis stands proudly against the blue sky. After exploring the archaeological site, unwind on the golden beaches or stroll through the charming village.

3. Marmaris, Turkey - A Taste of Asia:

- Crossing Borders: Take a ferry to Marmaris, Turkey, for a taste of cross-cultural exploration. Wander through bazaars, savor Turkish cuisine, and absorb the vibrant atmosphere of this coastal town.

Day Trip Recommendations

1. Boat Tour to Symi and Panormitis Monastery:

- Seafaring Odyssey: Embark on a boat tour to Symi and visit the Panormitis Monastery. Enjoy the azure waters, explore the monastery grounds, and soak in the charm of Symi's harbor.

2. Lindos Day Excursion:

- Time Travel to Lindos: Opt for a day excursion to Lindos, exploring its ancient acropolis, meandering through its white-washed streets, and basking in the Mediterranean sun on its idyllic beaches.

3. Turkish Delights in Marmaris:

- Cultural Journey: Experience a day trip to Marmaris for a taste of Turkish culture. Stroll through the Grand Bazaar, savor Turkish delights, and admire the blend of European and Middle Eastern influences.

Maximizing Your Day Excursions

1. Early Departures:

- Seize the Day: To make the most of your day trips opt for early departures. This ensures ample time to explore, discover, and soak in the beauty of each destination.

2. Guided Tours:

- Insider Insights: Consider guided tours for a deeper understanding of the history and culture of the places you visit. Knowledgeable guides can offer insights that enhance your overall experience.

3. Flexible Itineraries:

- Embrace Spontaneity: While it's good to have an itinerary, leave room for spontaneity. Serendipitous discoveries often lead to the most memorable moments.

4. Local Cuisine Sampling:

- Culinary Adventures: Delight in local cuisine during your day trips. Whether it's savoring Symian seafood or indulging in Turkish delicacies, let your taste buds be part of the journey.

Rhodes, with its strategic location in the Aegean, offers a myriad of day trip possibilities, each unveiling a new facet of this captivating region. Whether you choose the timeless beauty of Symi, the historical richness of Lindos, or the cross-cultural exploration in Marmaris, let each day trip be a chapter in your Aegean adventure. As you set sail or venture by land, embrace the anticipation of discovery, and let the enchantment of each destination leave an indelible mark on your journey.

Health and Safety

Ensuring your health and safety is paramount while savoring the beauty of Rhodes. From proactive measures to emergency preparedness, let this guide be your companion in navigating the island with confidence.

Staying Healthy While Traveling

1. Hydration and Sun Protection:

- Mediterranean Sun: Rhodes enjoys abundant sunshine. Stay hydrated and use sunscreen to protect yourself from the Mediterranean sun. Carry a reusable water bottle and reapply sunscreen throughout the day.

2. Local Cuisine Awareness:

- Culinary Exploration: While indulging in the local cuisine, be mindful of your food choices to prevent foodborne illnesses. Opt for bottled water and ensure that fruits and vegetables are properly washed.

3. Mosquito Protection:

- Nature's Inhabitants: In certain seasons, mosquitoes can be present. Use insect repellent, especially during evenings, and consider long sleeves and pants to minimize exposure.

Emergency Information

1. Emergency Numbers:

- Quick Access: Memorize or save emergency contact numbers. In Greece, the general emergency number is 112, and for medical emergencies, you can dial 166.

2. Embassy/Consulate Information:

- Assistance Abroad: Note the contact information for your country's embassy or consulate in Greece. They can provide assistance in case of lost documents, emergencies, or other unforeseen situations.

3. Travel Insurance:

- Coverage Assurance: Prioritize travel insurance that includes medical coverage.

Confirm the coverage details, including emergency evacuation if needed.

Medical Facilities on the Island

1. Rhodes General Hospital:
   - Primary Medical Center: Rhodes General Hospital, located in Rhodes Town, is the main medical facility on the island. It provides a range of medical services, including emergency care.

2. Pharmacies:
   - Accessible Healthcare: Pharmacies are scattered across Rhodes, offering over-the-counter medications and basic medical supplies. Check for local pharmacy hours and locations.

3. Private Clinics:
   - Specialized Care: In addition to the public hospital, there are private clinics on the island that cater to specific medical needs. They may provide faster service for non-emergency situations.

Health and Safety Tips

1. Stay Informed:

- Local Updates: Keep yourself informed about local health guidelines and updates, especially during your stay. Local authorities may provide information on potential health risks or safety measures.

2. Safe Exploration:

- Awareness is Key: Whether you're exploring ancient sites or enjoying the beaches, be aware of your surroundings. Follow safety guidelines at attractions and adhere to any warnings or advisories.

3. Travel with Essentials:

- First Aid Kit: Carry a basic first aid kit with essentials like bandages, pain relievers, and any personal medications you may need. Being prepared can alleviate minor health concerns.

Your journey in Rhodes is not just about the places you visit but also about safeguarding your well-being. By staying informed, taking proactive health measures, and being prepared for unforeseen situations, you can ensure a smooth and enjoyable experience on this enchanting island. Let health and safety be the silent companions of your Rhodes adventure, allowing you to focus on the wonders that await.

Local Customs and Etiquette

As you immerse yourself in the allure of Rhodes, understanding and respecting local customs and etiquette enhance not only your experience but also foster meaningful connections with the island's vibrant culture. Let this guide illuminate the nuances of Rhodesian traditions.

Understanding Rhodes Culture

1. Warm Hospitality:

- Embrace the Welcome: Rhodesians are known for their warm hospitality. Don't be surprised if locals engage in friendly conversations or offer assistance. Embrace this gesture, and reciprocate with a genuine smile.

2. Respect for Traditions:

- Cultural Richness: Rhodes boasts a rich cultural tapestry shaped by centuries of history. Respect local traditions, whether witnessed in festivals, religious ceremonies, or everyday life. Participate if invited, and observe with reverence.

3. Importance of Family:

- Family Bonds: Family holds immense importance in Rhodesian culture. It's common to see families gathering for meals and celebrations. If invited to a local home, consider it a privilege and express your gratitude.

Respectful Behavior for Visitors

1. Modest Attire in Religious Sites:

- Covering Up: When visiting churches or monasteries, dress modestly. Women should cover their shoulders, and men should avoid wearing shorts. Respect for religious spaces is deeply appreciated.

2. Greetings with Respect:

- Polite Interactions: In Rhodes, a handshake is a common form of greeting. Use polite expressions such as "kalimera" (good morning) and "kalispera" (good evening). A nod or slight bow may accompany greetings as a sign of respect.

3. Remove Shoes Indoors:

- Home Etiquette: If invited into a Rhodesian home, it's customary to remove your shoes upon entering. This practice aligns with a sense of cleanliness and respect for the household.

Cultural Do's and Don'ts

1. Do Sample Local Cuisine:

- Culinary Exploration: Embrace the opportunity to taste local dishes. It's a gesture of appreciation for Rhodesian gastronomy. Try specialties like moussaka, souvlaki, and local seafood.

2. Don't Disrupt Religious Ceremonies:

- Quiet Observation: If you chance upon a religious ceremony, maintain a respectful distance. Refrain from disrupting prayers or taking photos in sensitive areas. Observing quietly shows cultural sensitivity.

3. Do Bargain Politely:

- Market Etiquette: In markets, bargaining is a common practice. However, do so politely and with a sense of respect. It's about engaging in a friendly exchange rather than haggling aggressively.

4. Don't Point Feet:

- Foot Gesture Taboo: Avoid pointing your feet at people or religious icons. In Rhodesian culture, the feet are considered the lowest part of the body, and pointing them can be seen as disrespectful.

Rhodesian culture is a blend of ancient traditions and warm hospitality, creating a unique and welcoming atmosphere. By embracing local customs, respecting cultural nuances, and approaching interactions with an open heart, you'll find that Rhodesians reciprocate with genuine warmth. As you navigate this cultural tapestry, let respect be your compass, guiding you through the rich heritage and shared moments that make Rhodes a truly special destination.

Practical Tips

Embarking on a seamless journey through Rhodes involves a blend of insider advice, mindful budgeting, and staying connected. Let these practical tips be your compass, ensuring your time on the island is not just memorable but also effortlessly enjoyable.

Insider Advice for a Seamless Trip

1. Early Exploration:

- Beat the Crowds: To make the most of popular attractions like the Palace of the Grand Master, plan visits early in the morning. You'll enjoy a quieter experience and the enchanting morning light.

2. Local Transport Know-How:

- Navigating the Island: Opt for local transportation options like buses or taxis to explore the island. They are reliable and provide a glimpse into the daily life of Rhodesians. Plan your routes in advance for efficient travel.

3. Hidden Gems from Locals:

- Off-the-Beaten-Path: Strike up conversations with locals to discover hidden gems. Whether it's a secluded beach or a quaint village, the insights from those who call Rhodes home can lead to memorable discoveries.

Money Matters

1. Currency Exchange Tips:

- Best Rates: Exchange currency at banks or authorized exchange offices for better rates. Avoid airport kiosks for larger transactions. Notify your bank of your travel dates to avoid any issues with card transactions.

2. Cash and Card Balance:

- Mixed Approach: While cards are widely accepted, having some cash on hand is practical, especially in smaller establishments or markets. Ensure your cards are equipped for international transactions.

3. Budget for Excursions:

- Day Trip Considerations: If planning day trips, factor in additional expenses for transportation, meals, and activities. Having a budget specifically for excursions ensures you can make the most of your explorations.

Staying Connected on Rhodes

1. Local SIM Card:

- Cost-Effective Connectivity: Consider purchasing a local SIM card for your phone. It provides cost-effective data and ensures you stay connected, especially if you plan to use navigation apps or share your adventures in real time.

2. Internet Hotspots:

- Cafés and Public Spaces: Many cafés and public spaces offer free Wi-Fi. Enjoy a cup of Greek coffee while catching up on messages or sharing your favorite Rhodes moments with friends and family.

3. Emergency Contact List:

- Stay Prepared: Compile a list of emergency contacts, including local services, your embassy or consulate, and your accommodation details. Having this information readily available adds an extra layer of preparedness.

As you traverse the captivating landscapes and cultural wonders of Rhodes, these practical tips serve as your travel allies. Whether it's gaining insider insights, managing your finances wisely, or staying seamlessly connected, these nuggets of advice ensure that your journey is not only memorable but also marked by the ease that comes with thoughtful preparation. Bon voyage, and may your Rhodesian adventure be as smooth as the Aegean breeze!

Useful phrases

As you embark on your journey through the sun-kissed landscapes of Rhodes, a few well-chosen phrases can open doors and hearts. While many locals in tourist areas speak English, embracing a bit of the local language can enhance your experience and foster connections. Here are some essential phrases to help you navigate Rhodes with ease:

Greetings and Polite Expressions

Kalimera (Καλημέρα):

- Good morning: Begin your day with a warm greeting.

Kalispera (Καλησπέρα):

- Good evening: Use this phrase as the sun sets on your Rhodesian day.

Efharisto (Ευχαριστώ):

- Thank you: Express gratitude for a kind gesture or assistance.

Parakalo (Παρακαλώ):

- Please: Employ this polite term when making a request.

Ne (Ναι) / Ochi (Όχι):

- Yes / No: Simple yet crucial for clear communication.

Basic Conversation Starters

Poso kanei; (Πόσο κάνει;):

- How much is it?: Useful for shopping or negotiating prices.

Ti kanis; (Τι κάνεις;):

- How are you?: A friendly way to connect with locals.

Me lene (Με λένε):

- My name is: Introduce yourself with this handy phrase.

Ordering Food and Drinks

Tha thela ena... (Θα θέλα ένα...):

- I would like a...: Useful when ordering in restaurants or cafes.

Nero (Νερό):

- Water: Staying hydrated is essential, and this phrase ensures you get just that.

Efkharisto, to logariasmo parakalo (Ευχαριστώ, τον λογαριασμό παρακαλώ):

- Thank you, the bill please: Wrap up your meal with gratitude and a polite request.

Asking for Directions

Pos pao sto...; (Πώς πάω στο...;):

- How do I get to...? Handy for navigating your way around the island.

Aristera (Αριστερά) / Deksia (Δεξιά):

- Left / Right: Helpful for following directions.

Thelo na pao sto... (Θέλω να πάω στο...):

- I want to go to...: Specify your destination with this phrase.

Emergency Phrases

Boetheia! (Βοήθεια!):

- Help!: In case of an emergency, this word can be crucial.

Iatriko Kentro (Ιατρικό Κέντρο):

- Medical Center: Useful when seeking medical assistance.

Tha kliso to tilefono (Θα κλείσω το τηλέφωνο):

- I will call the police: Important in case of emergencies requiring police assistance.

Language Tips for Easy Communication

1. Learn Local Pronunciations:

- Embrace the Sounds: Greek has unique sounds. Pay attention to pronunciation, especially for words like souvlaki (soov-lah-kee) or tzatziki (dzah-DZEE-kee).

2. Practice Common Phrases:

- Daily Repetition: Practice common phrases regularly. Ordering coffee or asking for directions in Greek becomes a delightful part of your routine.

3. Use Simple Gestures:

- Universal Language: Complement your phrases with gestures. A smile, a nod, or a wave can enhance understanding and convey friendliness.

Enhancing Your Cultural Experience

1. Engage in Conversations:

- Friendly Interactions: Initiate conversations with locals using basic phrases. Even if you stumble, the effort is appreciated, and it often leads to delightful exchanges.

2. Explore Local Cuisine:

- Gastronomic Pleasures: When dining, ask for recommendations using Greek phrases. Locals often appreciate visitors embracing the local cuisine, and your efforts will be met with smiles.

3. Attend Cultural Events:

- Immersive Experiences: Attend local events or festivals where you can interact with residents. A few Greek phrases can make these cultural moments even more enriching.

Quick Tips:

1. Learn Numbers:

- Transaction Ease: Familiarize yourself with basic numbers for transactions. It simplifies shopping, ordering, and negotiating.

2. Ask for Language Help:

- Friendly Assistance: Don't hesitate to ask locals for help with pronunciation or understanding phrases. Greeks often enjoy helping language learners.

3. Travel Phrasebook Handy:

- Pocket-Sized Assistance: Carry a travel phrasebook for quick reference. It's a handy companion for moments when you need to express yourself or understand local responses.

These phrases, sprinkled with a warm smile, can transform your interactions on Rhodes. While English is widely understood, locals appreciate the effort to embrace their language. So, arm yourself with these expressions, dive into the cultural exchange, and let the language of Rhodes become part of your unforgettable journey. Kaló taxídi! (Καλό ταξίδι!) - Safe travels!

Conclusion

Congratulations, intrepid traveler, you've reached the final chapter of your virtual odyssey through the sun-drenched paradise of Rhodes! If this guide were a compass, you'd be pointing directly towards an adventure of a lifetime.

In these pages, we've unveiled the secrets of Rhodes, from the ancient wonders of the Old Town to the hidden gems tucked away in the island's nooks and crannies. You've been armed with practical tips to outsmart the crowds, navigate local lingo, and even bargain like a seasoned market pro. Whether you're a history buff exploring the medieval charm or a sun worshiper chasing those golden beaches, Rhodes has something for every wanderlust-infected soul.

As you bid adieu to this guide, remember: Rhodes isn't just an island; it's an emotion. It's the joy of tasting souvlaki under the Aegean sun, the wonder of gazing at ancient wonders, and the thrill of getting lost in its enchanting streets. We've packed this guide with all the essentials, but the real magic happens when you step out and create your own Rhodesian story.

And now, a little joke to send you off with a grin: Why did the tourist bring a ladder to Rhodes? Because they heard the views were on another level! Before you embark on your Rhodesian escapade, we want to express our heartfelt gratitude for choosing this guide. Your curiosity fuels our passion, and we're thrilled to have been your travel companion. We hope these pages have infused your journey with laughter, insights, and the unshakable desire to explore every nook and cranny of this island paradise.

As you venture forth, may your days be filled with sunshine, your nights with laughter, and your memories of Rhodes be as timeless as the beauty that surrounds you. Safe travels, fellow explorer, and may your adventures be as boundless as the horizon you're about to discover!